Simple Things Happiness

RK Cool Dude's Production

2022© RK Cool Dude

Simple Things for Happiness
Press

illustrated by various talented people

Visit Me Online:

https://www.amazon.com/author/rkcooldude

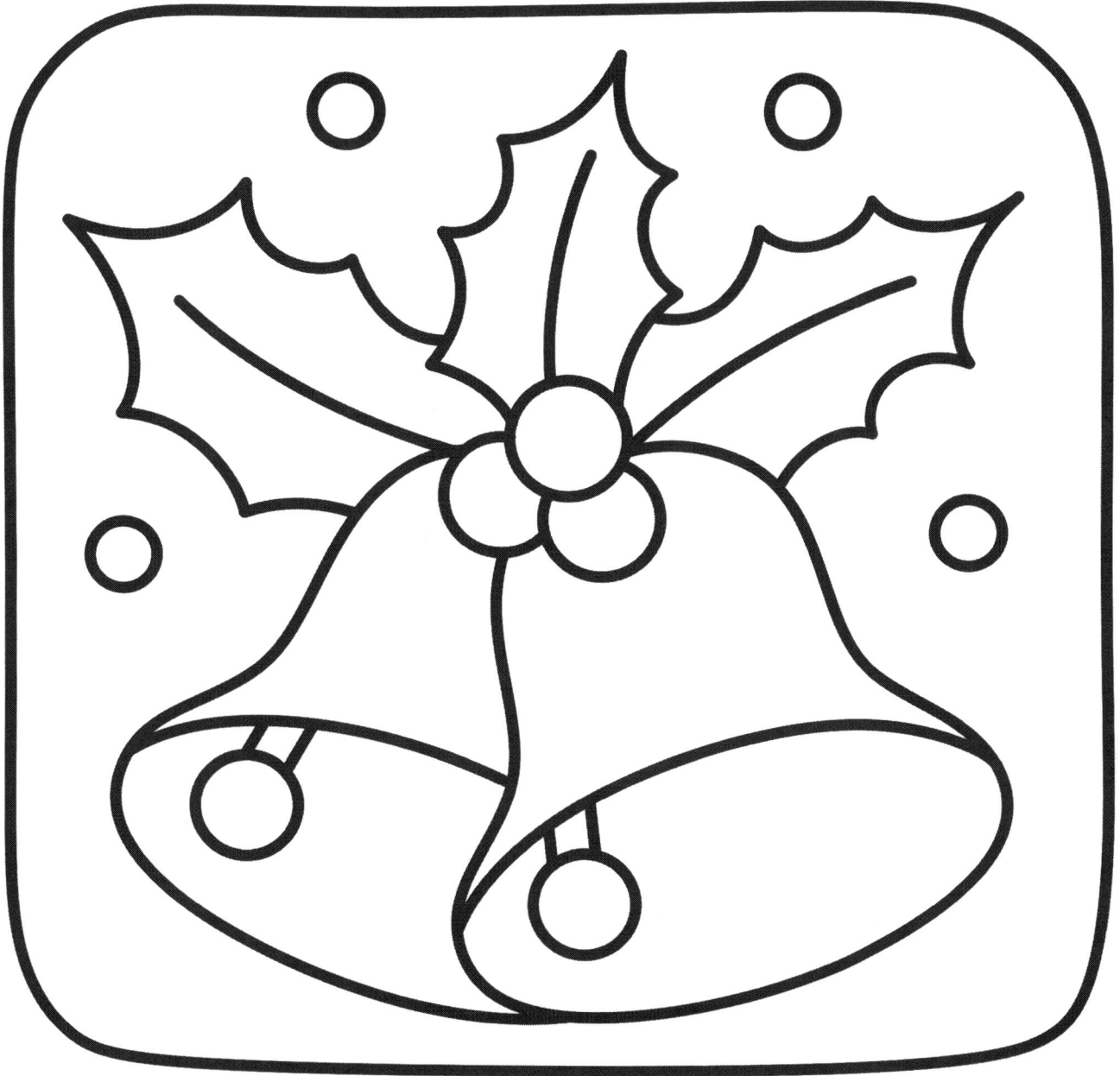

Printed in Great Britain
by Amazon

15501761R00061